It Don't Hurt Now

My Journey of Self-Love & Self-Acceptance

CHRISTIE A. CRUISE, PHD

DEDICATION

This book is dedicated to the loving memory of my brother, Donta. For all the times you protected me, thank you.

FOREWORD

"Can you read this over and give me your thoughts or feedback?" was a pretty simple question. Easy to answer, *"Of course!"* However, as I remembered what this book would be about, I was afraid to read even one page. I asked a co-worker to go for a walk with me, and that is *after* we had a drink. As I sat down, pen in hand, glasses perched to get started, I read through each sentence, then each page and only one question occurred to me over and over. *You, too?*

You see, dear reader, I met Christie in high school. We were not BFFs or anything like that, but we navigated the last year of high school, conversing over the silly adolescent thoughts one has at such an age. Had I known then that she was suffering the same emotional hell that I pretended did not exist in my own life night after night, would that have changed the course of my healing journey? Would it have changed hers?

Almost 20 years later, in an interview at my alma mater for a faculty position, I saw Christie at the table and breathed a sigh of relief to see a familiar face. Since that day in the cafeteria of my alma mater, we have shared the most intimate details of our lives while snacking, working on grant projects, snacking, forming a writing group, and snacking.

Thus, I already knew small parts of Christie's childhood story, and I supposed I just filled in the gaps with what I know to be true about growing up in America as a dark-skinned girl, now woman. But reading this book filled in the gaps between the gaps.

It Don't Hurt Now gives voice to the silenced group of little black girls and adult black women who have experienced colorism within our own racial group, and the emotional pain of questioning one's own beauty. This book gives voice to those silenced girls and women who have bodies that were violated by male monsters our families trusted. It gives voice to women taking on the challenge to learn how to have unconditional love for the body God gifted them.

Dr. Cruise is not only my friend; she is a writer, a Zumba instructor, and a shrewd self-employed businesswoman. She provides the inspiration to march to the beat of your own drum, but a healthy drum, a healthy march. Her story, her journey is filled with as much pain as it is filled with hope. Hope that tomorrow will bring the opportunity to make a new choice and chose our own selves and our own health over the happiness and comfort of undeserving others.

Within each section, you may find yourself asking aloud, *"You, too?"* as each line, each page confirms and validates reflections you thought only you experienced. Positive and negative events you thought only happened to you. For me, it was cathartic to read my own words coming from someone else's childhood trauma, someone else's journey to body acceptance, and the navigation of intimate relationships. This book is healing to those that have either repressed or suppressed the origins of their ruminating thoughts and self-doubt. Don't worry, by the end, you will feel empowered to hold your head up higher than yesterday, to speak louder and with more assertiveness in the next argument you have with a relative or partner, to challenge the status quo of what it means to be in love, and finally, to strengthen your relationship with self-acceptance.

I am a licensed professional counselor, educator, and researcher/writer and recommend this book to all dark-skinned girls and women; all sex abuse survivors (female, male, and non-binary identities), and the people that love them.

Namaste,

Dr. Shemya Vaughn, LPC, CRC

PREFACE

Journaling, for me, has always been a way to express myself. I find the practice cathartic and healing. I still have my very first diary from 1989. And, while my diary included the typical 13-year-old banter, it was mostly the conversation of a sad and lonely girl with her best friend; the diary.

I recognize that many of my journal excerpts, reflections, and poems in this book are not songs I sing alone. They are familiar for many. They are songs I sing with girls and women around the world. So, it is not only important for me to share my personal experiences of trauma and pain, but also for me to share my process for healing. A part of that process is journaling.

This book contains space for you, the reader, to reflect about your own experiences as they relate to each section. You may write as little or as much as you like, but please, write. If, while you are reading this book and/or reflecting on its contents, you begin to experience any distress and need to speak with someone, please know there are resources available to you.

National Suicide Prevention Lifeline
https://suicidepreventionlifeline.org/
1.800.273.8255

CONTACT Helpline
http://www.contacthelpline.org/
1.800.932.4616

Crisis Text Line
https://www.crisistextline.org/
TEXT HOME to 741741

Kids Under Twenty-One Crisis Helpline
http://kuto.org/
1.888.644.5886

The Trevor Lifeline
http://www.thetrevorproject.org/
1.866.488.7386

RAINN: National Sexual Assault Hotline
https://www.rainn.org/
1.800.656.4673

CONTENTS

ACKNOWLEDGMENTS

I would like to acknowledge the following people for their love, support, encouragement, shoulders, and ears: Malkia Davis, Tashiana Cheeks, Dr. Shemya Vaughn, Dr. Danielle Harris, Turan Mullins, Jarrett Fleming, and Darrick Hibbler. You are my village. Thank you for filling my cup.

I want to express my sincerest gratitude to Taylor Deed and Nyara Williams for their creative vision and direction. You work so beautifully together. You two were a God send.

I would like to thank my mentors Dr. Jenny Bloom and Dr. Charles Eberly. Dr. Eberly, I remember clearly during one of our meetings while I was working on my master's degree, you told me I had at least two good books in me. Dr. Bloom, when I visited you in South Carolina you encouraged me to write about my life. You said I had a story to tell. Thank you both for encouraging and believing in me.

And, to my countless friends and family who have loved me through the years, thank you.

INTRODUCTION

As far back as I can remember I have always loved music. It is from my mother that I inherited this love. She listened to almost every genre of music including jazz, R & B, rock, pop, blues, and gospel. When I was a little girl she would sit at the dining room table with a cigarette in one hand and a glass of beer in the other while I or my brother changed the albums on the record player based on her request. I'd sit on the floor, waiting for the next request, watching as she rocked back and forth, tapping her feet to the rhythm.

And, although I memorized the words to the songs of Luther Vandross, Shirley Brown, Journey, and the Rolling Stones, I had no idea, really, about what they were singing. It wasn't until I was in my early 20s and really began to listen to music, I mean really listen to it, that I understood the power of words and the comfort of a melody. Music speaks to our souls. It also speaks for us when we cannot find the words to express our feelings.

In 1978, Teddy Pendergrass released the song *It Don't Hurt Now* from the album *Life Is a Song Worth Singing*. I was three years old at the time and had no clue what Teddy was singing about. As an adult listening to this song, having experienced love and heartbreak, I understood the message he was trying to convey. We all experience hurt. The healing process, although necessary, can sometimes be more painful than the hurt itself. Once the healing process is complete, we are stronger because of the pain and wiser because of the process.

While Teddy was singing about healing from the hurt of an intimate relationship, the same principles can be applied to any process of hurt, letting go, and moving on. In my case, I had to unpack childhood hurt and trauma, and begin to process the issues impacting my self-esteem. Once I began that process, I started to feel better about myself. I guess like Teddy, I found a new relationship. I fell in love with me. The more I started to love me, the less I hurt. The more I embraced myself with all my flaws, the more the hurt started to fade. The more I shared my story about trauma, the less power the trauma had over me.

This book is a compilation of journal entries, reflections, and poems that have allowed me to speak to my pain, name it, and heal from it. It is about love and loss, trauma and healing, and growing and forgiving. It is my journey of healing through writing. I pray it is a blessing to others who have experienced trauma and are in search of peace. These writings helped heal my wounds. May they do the same for you.

1

DARK GIRLS DON'T CRY

They Just Internalize The Hurt Of A Color Conscious Society

TO BE DARK

"You are so cute to be dark!"

The first compliment I heard about my appearance was
also wrapped in an insult.

I wasn't sure what it really meant, but my soul did because
the words just sat in the pit of my stomach trying to digest,
but at the same time wanting to be expelled.

My beauty was shrouded in my skin; this skin that is dark as
night and represents all the fears of darkness.

Although the grandeur of the heavens is most appreciated
in the dark, there is still this unknown that exists that causes
folk to feel uncomfortable with it. It is as uncomfortable as
the lies we've been told about our inferiority.

And, although it makes no sense, we've accepted it; almost
like a prisoner on death row accepts his fate even when he
knows he's innocent.

Sometimes you can hear a lie so often that it smothers the
truth and becomes your reality.

Dirty, ugly, unworthy, unattractive, undesirable,
unintelligent, under appreciated.

This is what I was told as a child.

Yeah, you're smart, but you're a girl and your black.

Not just Black, but black.

I can see the pity when people look at me:
So sad. If only she were lighter, she'd at least have a chance.

At least she could be someone's wife; a Mrs.

Now, even that's farfetched.

What's her future? It is as dark as her skin.

Teen pregnancy? Yeah. You know what dark girls are good for.

The sex is tight, but a wife?

Perhaps they're right. Perhaps that's my calling, being used for the pleasures of others.

Don't ask for anything in return. Be grateful for what you got.

He's gonna leave anyway, but if you're quiet maybe he'll want to come back, you know, when he has no other place to go.

You'll be here waiting.

What else do you have?

Dark skin. Ah, now I remember why he can't make me his wife.

His family wants to lighten the gene pool and you just won't do.

Slow down dark girl, stay in your place.

Now, even when a man truly desires you because he sees your beauty, the lies you've been fed will eat away at your confidence and your soul until even his love can't silence what you've been told.

You'll doubt, questioning his intentions because now you've internalized the self-hate that was passed on to you from other victims of circumstance.

So now what? How do you unpack this bag you've carried on your back and in your spirit and in your heart for so long?

Where do you even begin?

Cry little black girl. Just cry.
Cry and release the lies you've been told.

Allow your eyes to do what, for so long, your soul couldn't do.

Release.
Let it go.

You are stronger than that who they tried to make you.
You are smarter than that who they tried to have you believe you were.

This is your dawn.

Awake into your full self, the being of light that God created.

AND IF YOU FEEL THIS WAY...

The things you said to me, I can't believe that's what you think of me.

I'm a black bitch.

An ape.

An ugly black slut.

A monkey.

I expect to hear those things from other people, I've heard it most of my life.

But you, you're my blood.

And, if you feel this way, what must others think of me. Am I so unlovable, so repulsive?

What did I say to you to make you speak to me in this way?

Have you always felt this way?

The times when I shared my deepest hurts about how my skin was a constant source of pain for me, did you secretly agree with my tormentors?

It seems you did.

Why else would you repeat words that are like razors to my welted chocolate skin?

Words that haunted me most of my childhood.

Words that, as a teenager, I'm just starting to relinquish as part of my identity.

How could you hurt me in this way?

No one else said anything to stop you.

Were they just in shock? I know I was.

I'm sorry I hit you in your face. That was my reaction to the hurt you inflicted on me.

My fight or flight kicked in and I decided to fight.

I wanted to hurt you as much as you hurt me.

The beating I inflicted on you eventually came to an end, and the scars will heal.

But, the beating your words inflicted on my heart and mind will stay for a lifetime.

Eventually, these feelings will subside, and I will add them to the pile of hurts I will eventually have to work through.

Thanks for your contribution.

KIDS DON'T TAKE AFTER STRANGERS

"Kids can be so cruel", I've heard it said.

Shit, so can grown folk.

The reality is that kids take their lead from adults.

Where did these kids learn to be so cruel and use such scathing language: crispy, blacky, tar baby, black bald-headed bitch, darky, dirt?

I'll wait.

Right.

They heard you describe your cousin or sister that way.

They listened to their brother's friend describe the next-door neighbor in that way while you laughed instead of interrupting such toxic talk.

Truth is, you agree.

You feel that way about me and more importantly you feel that way about yourself.

Why else would you allow such words to be uttered in your presence to describe a woman who shares a common experience as you?

What made you believe it was appropriate to perpetuate the very stereotypes that have plagued a people marginalized by the very society that appropriates their culture in the name of capitalism?

You didn't think it was that deep, huh?

You too have internalized the racism and sexism that has become so commonplace as the American Way.

INTERNALIZED HURT

"He probably doesn't date black women, and if he does, he probably doesn't date dark-skinned black women."

Those are always my first thoughts when I see black men I find attractive.

I don't even give myself a chance to move past that point nor do I even continue with whatever eye contact we started.

"He's probably looking past me. Maybe he's just smiling to be nice."

I've heard it so much. "I don't date dark-skinned women", "I just am not attracted to dark-skinned girls", "I just think I look better with light-skinned or white girls."

These are the recordings that play over and over in my head.

These are the realities of this dark girl.

Internalized rejection.

Internalized colorism.

Internalized oppression.

Have I gotten better? Yes.

I've learned to love the skin I'm in even if no one else

does.

But, those recordings, they're hard to turn off.

Press stop.

Eject.

Erase.

Delete.

But, telling this story helps unburden me of the shame and the hurt.

The recordings will wane. I know. They already have.

UNTITLED
(YOU ARE BEAUTIFUL)

You are beautiful.

No one knows, though.

Behind that shroud of darkness, you are beautiful.

They can't see. Your skin stops them from going deeper.

Never getting to listen to your thoughts, hear your laughter, share your dreams.

It's like they're looking through you.

You're invisible.

No reflection.

Just breath, nothing more than air taking up space.

You are beautiful.

No one cares, though.

Your skin isn't on the checklist of beautiful things.

There's no need to go deeper.

The stereotypes and internalized oppression have defined you.

They know all they need to know.

Unattractive, unintelligent, uninteresting, undesirable, undeserving.

ALL MINE

This skin.

My pain.

My hurt.

My burden.

I carry this.

It's heavy.

Only so far, I can go before my feet, my heart, my head needs solace.

A place.

It looks familiar.

Yes, it's where dark girls rest.

At the intersection of Hurt Street and Reject Boulevard.

I won't stay here.

My destiny is greater than this.

This place where you try to hold me and diminish my existence to the pigment of my flesh.

My soul is greater than that because my creator is greater than that.

I am the universe, His image, beautifully and fearfully made.

You don't have it.

My power.

I reclaimed it.

Goodbye.

14

APPROPRIATION

These lips, these eyes, this butt, these thighs, never enough with this chocolate skin. White or light skin, now it's in.

Waiting to be Needed

My childhood, like my skin, so dark.

Feeling out of place everywhere.

Invisible until I do something wrong or something right that benefits the needs of others...going to the store for cigarettes and soda, stepping in to a competition when your first choice isn't prepared.

I'm everything now. Hoist me up on your shoulders.

This celebration isn't even sweet. It's all too familiar.

When I no longer suit your purpose, I'll disappear into the night. Dark like my skin.

Won't be missed. I don't exist. Not until the next time you need a third for whatever game or someone to go pick up the Chinese food.

And, I'll go. Just to be a part of something. Just for a minute of visibility. Fleeting. It's better than nothing, I suppose. I wouldn't know.

JOURNAL ENTRY
DECEMBER 11, 2004

Today I struggled in my mind and heart with the lives people live and why.

As I sit in church I notice the people and can see their struggles.

From knowing one part of their lives I can imagine their struggles.

Mostly, though, I sympathize. I can feel their hurts, confusion, and fears.

I too have hurts, confusions, and uncertainties about life and fears.

I'm afraid I'm not good enough professionally and spiritually.

I fear I may never get married and have children, although this fear has become more of an acceptance of my possible fate.

I'm confused about my purpose in life.

I'm hurt by how I've allowed people to treat me and how I subsequently treat myself.

I've become someone I no longer know. I wonder if they feel the same.

I wonder if they, too, have lost themselves.

HEALING

This time, no picking off the scab of wounds of old to heal.

This time, I only need look at the scars to close this chapter.

That's progress.

ARRIVING AT LOVE

It's taken me this long.

I look in the mirror at this chocolate skin and I smile.

It's beautiful.

I can remember a time when I looked in the mirror with such disappointment; sadness.

But, no more.

I'm beautiful.

My skin, my hair, my lips, all of me.

I look at my body; my chocolate body.

It's beautiful.

This smooth, creamy dark chocolate skin is beautiful.

I touch my thighs, my arms, my breast, all of me

I'm in love!

To think I believed those lies

I almost let them destroy me.

I didn't know those lies were created out of jealousy,

Desire for this beautiful skin.

All this melanin,

Sun-kissed skin,

Beautiful,

Chocolate,

Me!

2

IF THESE LABIA COULD TALK

The Untold Stories Of My Vagina

EMPTY

Hollow, empty, space...my womb; barren, no fruit, no life, no legacy; gone.

My existence ends with me.

I hope they know.

I was here.

I was present.

No one to tell my story.

No branches for the tree.

The last leaf has fallen.

And, when the wind blows it will fly away.

Will it be remembered?

When I Let Go

I was trying so hard to hold on to something that was killing me. Heavy bleeding every month, painful cramps, nausea, diarrhea, fatigue, anemia. Even with all that, I still couldn't bring myself to do it. It's one thing to decide you don't want children. It's another thing altogether when you don't have a choice.

But still I couldn't let go. Endometriosis, fibroid tumors covering most of my uterus. A uterus so enlarged that my right ovary can't be seen on the ultrasound. But still, I just couldn't let go. Abdominal pain from ovarian cysts. Pain so severe that my legs can't be still. Nose bleeds, migraines, cold fingers and toes, and I still couldn't let go.

Worsening depression and anxiety, emotional, and a loss of a desire to do anything. Inability to take long trips without multiple restroom breaks all because I couldn't let go. When I finally let go and had the hysterectomy I was crushed.

After my body healed from surgery, that first month without a period was bliss. Why in the hell did I hold on to so much pain for so damn long? I'll tell you why. I believed that my womanhood was tied to my uterus and my ability to have children.
Now I know, I am still a woman!
I am a woman with a better quality of life.
I am a healthy woman.

I am a woman!
I am a woman!
I AM a woman!

WOMAN TO WOMAN

Do you have children?
You don't? Why not?
Don't you want children?
Every woman wants children?
But you would make such a good mom?
Doesn't your mom want some grand babies?
Who's going to take care of you when you get old?
Doesn't your husband want children?
You're not getting any younger!
You better do it now while you still have the energy.
Being a mom is what defines you as a woman.
Being a mom is the most important thing you'll ever do.

Listen!
Stop limiting my existence as a woman to bearing children.
Don't ask me personal questions about my body.
Mother or not I am a woman. Don't define me by my
ability or lack thereof to give birth.
Don't question my choice to have or not to have children.
Respect me as a woman and love and support me because
we are sisters.
Love me for who I am just as I love you for who you are.
Stop! Please.

I Don't Know Who I Am

Gaining weight saved my life.

It looked unhealthy, even disgusting to most, but it was the healthiest thing for me.

No more cat calls, no more fear of being touched by neighbors and school boys and teenagers.

I was safe.

It is terrible for a child to have to choose between her safety and her weight, but I did.

I chose my safety.

My mother didn't understand when she'd yell at me about getting fat.

My brother didn't understand when he was embarrassed of his little sister because she was putting on so much weight.

My sisters didn't understand when they didn't want to take me shopping because all the cute clothes came in smaller sizes.

The neglect and invisibility at home just added to the depression and feeling of emptiness.

The food filled those voids.

It filled the void of not being good enough; the void of not being pretty enough or being perceived as not being smart enough.

The food filled the void and the emptiness of my soul.

It filled me and filled me and filled me until I didn't recognize myself.

My body was someone else's; someone who wasn't desirable.

I hated her, but I needed her.

I knew without her I was at risk of being violated by every perverted man and boy in our neighborhood.

I accepted her and lost myself in her until we became one.

Better to willingly lose myself in her than to lose myself unwillingly in them.

I was lost nevertheless.

MY POWER

This is the second time your kind thought you had permission to use my vagina as a toy; a Rubik's cube or some Play-Doh.

Maybe those toys enjoyed your hand exploring its depths, but I don't.

My 8-year-old vagina didn't like it any more than my 38-year-old vagina.

Who told you it was okay to touch me there?

To probe into my womanhood as if it were part of your right as a human being.

What made you think you had my permission to touch my private parts?

Perhaps my sitting here innocently on my front porch playing led you to believe I wanted what you did to me.

Maybe it was me coming to your establishment for my regular massage that gave you the impression that I wanted your fingers in my vagina.

My bad. I didn't know.

I didn't know there was something seductive about playing on my front porch at 8 years old.

I didn't know regular massages with you meant I wanted something more, a happy ending.

I didn't know if I told I'd be interrogated like a criminal, have my integrity questioned, and have my childhood trauma on display.

I mean, it's not like you were raped.

He only stuck his fingers in your pussy, right? Right? It's not like you haven't had somebody's fingers in your pussy before.

Didn't your neighbor do the same thing when you were 8 years old? You were alright, right? Look at you! You're a doctor! You turned out alright, so it couldn't have been that traumatic! You're not on drugs. You're not out tricking. It could've been a lot worse. You know?

Yeah, I know. I told myself those lies too when I didn't understand the power I was relinquishing by being silent.

Your hands hurt me. They took a piece of me, but I will not allow them to silence me.

You will not take my power. You will not cover my mouth and strangle my truth.

This is not my shame! This is not my burden. My truth shall make me free!

THE LONG WALK HOME

School bell rings.

The walk home starts as a time to laugh, joke, play, run.

It's all fun until right around 23rd Street at the corner stoop.

Old men, young men, life had passed them by while they're shooting the shit on that stoop.

Me and my friends we know what time it is.

We hold on tight to the straps of our backpacks, ready to run for our lives if need be.

We start out with a hesitant walk. No eye contact.

We're talking, but not really; trying to listen to what they're saying.

Then it starts.

"Hey girl. Come here. I ain't gone do nothing to you."

Our steps grow quicker.

"Damn, look at that ass."

One of the men gets up from the stoop and begins walking toward us.

We don't wait. We run.

Sometimes they don't chase. Sometimes they do.

Sometimes we get away. Sometimes we don't.

On a good day. We run home, out of breath, but intact.

On a bad day like today, they chase, and one of us gets caught.

Today was my turn.

When he grabs my arm, I yell for him to stop and to let me go.

He's not listening because his hands are in my shirt, on my behind, squeezing and rubbing.

He finally let go. I walk home embarrassed and ashamed; dirty and disgusted.

"I hate them." I utter to myself, chin shaking because I want to cry.

"You alright?" My friend who got away asks.

"Yeah." I change the subject.

Maybe tomorrow I won't get caught.

No Interest

I have no interest in hearing what you have to say, how beautiful I am, how good I smell, and how soft my body feels.

I have no interest in sitting on your face or having your penis penetrate my soul, your hands between my legs, or your tongue in my mouth.

I have no interest in hearing how you can't control yourself when you're in my presence.

You seem confused by the nonchalant look on my face while you kiss my breast and thighs in an attempt to get me wet.

The truth is, you just don't get it. You don't get how my heart has been broken and my body used for the pleasure of others.

You don't understand that I've given my all to relationships that weren't worth all the work it took to put the pieces back together.

You don't understand that in love there is no separation of the heart and the body.

So, no, I'm not interested. I'm not interested in having my emotions toyed with for your amusement, or my vagina entered for your pleasure.

I am not interested in your excuses when you stop calling with the frequency with which you once did. Or in you making promises to me that you have no intention to keep.

No thanks. I'll keep my heart, soul, and body intact. I'm sorry. I'm just not interested in you.

UNTITLED
(MY VIRGINITY)

I used to define myself by my virginity; like it somehow made me better because I still had it.

I may have been violated, but at least I hadn't been penetrated. That was important to me. I felt like it was all I had; like it was the only thing that made me special.

I held on so tight to it that the thought of losing it caused anxiety. If I lost it then what did I have to make me special, more importantly, who was I without it.

What would happen to me if I couldn't use as an excuse to keep from being intimate with men that I was waiting until marriage?

That's when I discovered the true source of my anxiety: intimacy. It was never really about my virginity. It was about my fear of being intimate-bearing my soul to someone, allowing myself to be vulnerable.

It took me until 29 years of age to begin the process of working through my insecurities and my fears and to lose my virginity.

It took me that long to feel comfortable about being vulnerable and to find my strength through my vulnerability. I'm still working through the process. Intimacy, though something I desire, is sometimes difficult for me. I realize now, though, that it's only a portion of what I contribute to a relationship. I understand that I am so much more and am not defined by it.

It Don't Hurt Now

I can relax and breathe and be my own woman.

I choose how I will be defined.

MY BODY'S SECRETS

You always tell me you want to see me naked;
You are so carefree with your body.

You show me every part of you, no reluctance, no fear.
You're beautiful. Your confidence, your smile, your skin,
your manliness is beautiful.

Where did that come from?
Were your private parts never caressed by your neighbor
when you were a child?

Was your body never a source of anxiety?
Were you never afraid of being touched inappropriately by
the opposite sex when you were a child?

Have you never used food to distort your soul and body to
encapsulate you for safety?
Those were my fears. That was my reality. My body bares
those scars.

If I reveal my body to you will you see them?

Will you be as disgusted by it as I sometimes am when I
think of my body's journey?

Can you handle its secrets? Sometimes I can't.

I want to share all of me with you, but I'm afraid.

Hold out your hands. Be gentle. She's fragile.

THE THINGS THEY SAY

I went through my contacts today and deleted every man in my phone who I know means me no good.

I'm smart enough to know and I've been around long enough to know when a man is just interested in sex.

Like when we first meet and the only thing you can do is look at my ass. You just want sex.

Or when your conversation has no substance, but you want to know when we gone hookup. Sex.

When you can't keep your hands off my thighs and my ass and we haven't got to the location for our date. Sex.

When you say you want to "fuck with" me. Sex.

When I ask what book you've read lately, and you respond, "Shit, I'm trying to read you". Sex.

When you just want to come over to my house and chill and talk and we haven't gone out on a date or even had a whole conversation. Sex.

When I tell you to send me a text to confirm some information and you say you don't really text. Not only do you want sex, but you're cheating!

It's time for me to grow up.

I need to stop entertaining nonsense.

If nonsense is where you dwell, nonsense is what you'll get.

I value my time and my body more than that.

3

MAKE IT STOP

Ongoing Struggles
With Depression and Anxiety

THE FIRST TIME

My first time…my first time was 8th grade.

I was so nervous. At the same time, though, I felt relief.

I knew it was going to hurt, but I wanted to do it anyway. I wanted it to be quick.

I went back and forth about doing it.

"I don't want to go to hell" I remember thinking.

It was too late, though, I was already in hell.

The constant jokes about my clothes, my hair…I was miserable.

The people in the movies always slice their wrists. I could do that.

Even then, the researcher in me wanted to do a pilot study. I started with my fingers.

The first finger I cut, I knew I couldn't tolerate the pain long enough to slice wrists.

What's plan B? I could throw myself in front of one of those 18-wheel trucks.

That's a two for one. I can die and save my soul.

But, when the day came, my conscience got the best of me.

Could I really allow someone to live with that type of trauma?

I couldn't do it.

That was my first time.

It wasn't my last.

Longing for Rest

I just lay there.

Eyes open, aware.

Discontent with waking up.

Heart racing, stomach weak, body tired.

Why?

I can't do this.

I want to lay here forever.

Not just here, but in an eternal sleep.

Forever asleep.

No sadness, no anxiety, no depression, just nothingness.

Empty.

Void.

Absent.

Me.

Let me go.

Let me be.

Let me rest.

The darkness has to be better than this.

Better than constant tears, feelings of inadequacy, fear and

panic.

The darkness of death has to provide peace from this.

I long for that rest.

LACK

The holes in our roof are many, like the holes in my soul
Rain making its way in, tapping in the pots on the floor
Rhythmic
Like the pain my heart feels from the dark clouds of
poverty
Each drop a reminder of what I am not and the lack I
inherited

Drown me in those drops
Drown my sorrows and hurt
Drown my body and soul
Drown my love and joy
Immerse all that I am not in those pots
Let it all wash away
Let it overflow
Until those pots are empty
And reflective of my lack

JOURNAL ENTRY
OCTOBER 2016

Eating to numb my pain isn't exactly new for me.

It's what I know. It's what I've always done to comfort myself from the ills of life and the world around me.

Reflecting on why I'm eating to numb the pain is a new concept for me, though.

As I sat, yet again, numbing my pain by popping chocolate, I asked myself, "What are you really eating?"

With each piece I ate, I verbally stated what it represented.

Today I realized I was eating loneliness, low self-esteem, frustration with my living situation, my inability to travel like I desire.

I ate sadness, feelings of inadequacy, stress, and disappointment.

I ate childhood trauma, family dysfunction, and secrets.

I ate until I disappeared inside myself.

I ate until the serving size on that bag of chocolate became a recommendation for those who give a damn.

I ate until I cried because I wasn't sure what to do with all that I'd unpacked in that moment.

I decided to write about it to help me process it all. So that's what I'm doing, and it's helping.

JOURNAL ENTRY
JANUARY 2010

January 1:

Last night around the same time as tonight, I seriously considered checking myself into a psychiatric facility. I wanted to harm myself.

Right now, though, while my anxiety is still quite high, I feel somewhat calmer. I mean, I don't feel like I want to hurt myself now.

It's interesting how the thought of suicide can come and go so quickly. I know I need to be in therapy. I know I need to be on medication, but I can't afford either.

January 2:

And just like that, my thoughts of hurting myself have come back. I guess the early morning has become my enemy.

It's 2am, and instead of lying in bed I'm sitting in the kitchen writing to keep my mind off the knife on the counter that looks really tempting.

I already ran it across my stomach and both wrists, scratching the surfaces, but not actually breaking the skin. I think the only thing that keeps me from going through with it is my mother.

I saw how she grieved when my brother passed away. I know she wouldn't recover from this one. I can't do that to her.

If I could sleep; if my mind could quiet down I know these thoughts of suicide would diminish. At least that's what I hope.

JOURNAL ENTRY
JULY 2005

Have you ever wished you could go back in time and do parts of your life over?

Have you ever wished you could change decisions you made?

Sometimes I wish I could do just that. I know it's not possible, though. So, now what? So, now I sit here and wait for the sun to come up.

I haven't been up this early since last summer when I was having panic attacks. Subsequently, I haven't felt this empty since then either.

In my struggle to find myself, what I'm finding is that I would rather not exist.

Everybody thinks I have it all together. They have no idea.

My professor told me I was an excellent student. God knows that's what I strive for. My friends think I'm wonderful, and God knows I try to be.

But, there is still a part of me that's broken and searching for something.

What is it that I'm searching for? What happens when I find it? What if I'm still broken at the end of my search? What will I do then?

And there begins the anxiety; what if, what if, what if? Then, I feel like I'm losing control. I calm myself down, but the cycle will soon repeat. It always does. I'm exhausted.

JOURNAL ENTRY
JUNE 2005

Last year around this time I was struggling badly mentally and emotionally.

I could feel myself slipping back into depression and I wanted to die. I remember thinking that I didn't want to live with myself anymore. I was so tired of being me.

I would lie in bed and feel so isolated from the world. My mind was often filled with constant, crazy thoughts that wouldn't let me rest.

I'm a terrible person.

I'm not right.

What's wrong with me?

Maybe I have a brain tumor.

These thoughts made me question if there was really something going wrong with my brain.

I had begun having terrible nightmares; paralyzing ones. The images were so real!

I wasn't afraid as much as I was frustrated that I had no control. I felt so empty and dysfunctional. I felt out of place. I just wanted to die!

Today, in therapy, as I reflected on that time in my life I realized how fragile we are as human beings.

I realized the impact our childhoods have on our mental wellbeing as adults.

I realized my desire for perfectionism is a result of never feeling good enough as a child.

I still feel vulnerable and lonely like that little girl on 21st Street.

What makes us who we are? Is it our past experiences that shape us? Is it genetics?

My mother has shared with me on a few occasions that she

was extremely depressed when she was pregnant with me.
She was always anxious and afraid because my dad was
physically and emotionally abusive.

I often wonder if her experiences with depression and
anxiety were passed on to me in her womb.

In the end, does it really matter? My therapist thinks so, and
I trust her.

MYTHS AND STEREOTYPES

I hate that myth of the strong Black woman. I hate what that myth has done to us. We have been silenced by that myth.

We aren't allowed to be depressed or have anxiety. We aren't allowed to be vulnerable or sad. We aren't allowed to cry or be angry.

Because with the myth of the strong Black woman has also come the stereotype of the angry Black woman.

Either way, we are never truly able to express ourselves.

The result? We hold it all inside until it becomes like septicemia poisoning our blood.

If we are angry it's because we make sacrifices that no one acknowledges or appreciates. We are pissed off because we have allowed pieces of ourselves to die to satisfy people who didn't give a damn about us to begin with.

We are not strong because we want to be; we are strong because we have to be. We are a hurt people. We have been neglected and betrayed. We have been used and exploited. We have been appropriated and acculturated.

Now, what we need most, is to be healed and to be loved.

JOURNAL ENTRY
JUNE 2, 2005

On Tuesday my therapist asked me to think of a metaphor or an analogy that describes my life now, and if I am unhappy with it, think of one I'd like to describe it instead. I immediately thought about this dream I have regularly where I'm in another country and I'm driving over an old bridge. There's a terrible storm causing the water below the bridge to roar and splash with great force.

I must drive through the horrible conditions on the bridge to make it to my destination. Although I'm afraid the water will overtake my vehicle and I'll drown, I take the risk because it's the only way. I always make it across safely, but the dream is scary nonetheless. That is a perfect description of how I feel about my life. I don't like that at all.

I would prefer the description be of a beautiful park with lovely flowers and trees near the lake. I see myself sitting on a swing relaxing while I peacefully enjoy God's creation. The sound of nature is so peaceful and calm.

Then, my therapist asked me something; something I had never considered. She asked, "What would happen if you waited for the storm to calm before crossing the bridge?" I sat there for a moment. It was so simple, but so profound. Truth is, I never thought about that as an option. I was so used to things in my life being difficult that the thought had never crossed my mind. I felt empowered when I left. I have more control over my life than I realized.

MY DEPRESSION
(FROM CURVACEOUSLY FIT & HEALTHY BLOG)

It was on one of my many flights to some location in the US that I heard the phrase that would change my life. "Please securely place the oxygen mask over your nose and mouth before assisting children or others with theirs."

I've heard this phrase since I took my first flight in 1995. However, it was 20 years later, on a flight to Florida that this statement clicked and a light bulb came on in my head. That was my problem. I was so busy putting the oxygen mask on those around me that I had neglected to ensure I was able to breathe.

It's been over a decade since I was diagnosed with Major Depressive Disorder and Generalized Anxiety Disorder. When I was initially diagnosed I had mixed emotions. I felt embarrassed, relieved and sad. But, I wasn't surprised. At the time I was diagnosed I was already familiar with the feelings I had been experiencing over the past year. I had been experiencing these feelings since elementary school. However, in the 1980s, many people didn't believe children could suffer from depression. Also, I was a black child in the inner city with no health insurance and from a culture where you "don't put your business in the street".

By the time I was an adult I had mastered the art of coping with depression, mostly by overeating. In 2004, I was going about my life working, serving in church and in my community, being a good friend, daughter and sister when I reached a point where my old coping mechanisms were no longer effective. So, I met with my then primary care physician and finally came clean about how I had been feeling over the past several months, and most of my life. He suggested that I begin regular therapy and start taking anti-depressants. And, even though I knew in my heart I needed both, I decided to only seek therapy.

Eventually, my mental health declined, and I suffered a major panic episode that lasted for over 24 hours. Due to the severity of this panic episode, my doctor made it clear to me that not taking the medication was no longer an option. I began taking anti-depressants and continued in therapy and soon began to get better. But there was this part of me that was embarrassed that I couldn't function without medication. I felt damaged. I rarely spoke of my therapy and medication because I knew how some of my family members felt about both.

Again, I continued to work and work and give and give. In January 2015 I found myself in the emergency room where the doctor told me I would need to stay in the hospital because some of my test came back abnormal and there were some concerns. As I lay in the hospital bed, alone in my room, I felt a sense of peace. I felt safe and for the first time in a long time, I felt as though it was okay for me to rest. So, I did. Three days in the hospital. When the cardiologist informed me that all my tests came back normal and that stress from my life; my work and my family had most likely caused many of the symptoms I had been experiencing over the past few weeks, I knew it was time for a change. Once I was released from the hospital I followed up with my primary care physician. She adjusted my medication and we discussed ways in which I could decrease stress in my life.

Exercise is one way I destress, and travel is another. I decided to take some time off for myself. Then, I was on a flight when the flight attendant said those words, and it dawned on me. I had been putting the oxygen mask on everyone else, my husband, my job, my family, but had neglected to secure the mask over my own nose and mouth. The result, my mind and body hit a wall and I ended up in the hospital. It was during that plane ride that I decided that if I am going to truly be healthy and happy, my body couldn't be the only area of my life I focused on getting fit and healthy. I needed to put in some work in to developing a healthy mind and spirit.

My name is Dr. Christie Cruise and I have been diagnosed with clinical depression and anxiety disorder. I take medication daily and attend therapy once a week. I work out regularly to help find balance in my life and I have begun making lifestyle changes that allow me to take care of myself; mind, body and spirit.

I am no longer ashamed or embarrassed. I feel empowered and mentally fit and healthy.

4

THE NAKED TRUTH

Body
Image

THE DUALISM OF INVISIBILITY

Wanting to be seen but, wanting to disappear.

Swaddle Me

My body image was shaped early in my life by what others thought of me.

I knew there was something 'womanly' about my body, and I didn't like it.

Conversations about my body and how I would be 'built' like my mother were embarrassing to say the least.

Covering my backside by wrapping shirts and jackets around my waist in the presence of family and friends became my norm.

I often wished I was in a cocoon. I wanted to have a little girl's body. I wanted smaller legs, thinner thighs, a smaller behind. I wanted to wear rompers and short shorts with tank tops.

There was safety in having a little girl's body, or at least I thought.

I surely didn't know the depths of the perverseness of men who sexualized children's bodies. I didn't know that regardless of my 'shape', there were adults who were pedophiles.

Because I didn't understand this, I internalized their depravity. I made their issues my own.

The cocoon I created for myself swaddled me in excess weight. My body went through its own metamorphosis, but a butterfly I did not become.

What I became was an afraid little girl who went from disliking her body to absolutely loathing it.

That little girl still exists. She shows up now and again, and I calm her. I swaddle her. Sometimes with food, but most times with love and affection and affirmation of her right to exist and to be safe. And, more importantly, to be a little girl.

America's Body

My body is not really my own.

If it were, I wouldn't be concerned with what others think about it.

Engaging in fitness trainings knowing my body is injured, Not taking it easy and pushing my body to the limit. I know better.

But, I was the only plus sized woman in the training and the only woman of color.

I know what people think about women of color, especially black women.

They think we're all fat and out of shape; that we don't care about our bodies, about our health.

So, to debunk a stereotype I did things to my body in that training that I knew I'd pay for later.

I ran on the treadmill and did high intensity interval training, jumping over ramps knowing that my back and hips couldn't take that type of work on my body, but I did it.

I felt like I had to, like I was defending the honor of all black women across the country.

I defended our right to be curvy and healthy.

I defended our right to exist in a world that thinks we're less than.

I defended our bodies, bodies that have been abused more than they have been loved; that have nursed other women's children, cooked their food and cleaned their homes.

I defended bodies that have been raped, abused, abandoned, and rejected.

Bodies off which the backs of this nation were built and sustained long before there was a woman's movement and her right to work.

We were working, building, fighting, crying, hurting, but still moving forward; moving our families forward, sometimes alone.

Now, our bodies are exploited, appropriated for capitalism; we have been reduced to a trend.

Our braided hair which made it easier for us to pick your cotton, our curvy hips and large behinds, which bore the children of our rapists, once a source of criticism, is now a desire of all women.

This body never was my own. It's always belonged to others, subject to the criticisms of others.

But, no more. We are empowered; learning to love what others have rejected. Self-love is incredible. It will drown out the noise of a cruel society. It will heal us. We are celebrating what is naturally ours; what is naturally beautiful.

BROKEN FROM THE INSIDE OUT

I know I must go, but it causes me so much anxiety.

Doctor's appointments just remind me of all the things wrong with me...

Multinodular goiter

Uterine fibroids

Endometriosis

Benign masses in my breasts

Depression

Anxiety

Obesity

Fatigue

Sleep apnea

I feel like a freak of nature,

Like my body has and continues to betray me.

I feel broken inside.

I feel like a package that was opened in the store, its contents removed, prodded, and unwanted, balled up and put back in the package, in no way resembling its original state.

Now, the skin I'm in, my wrapping, reflects the brokenness I feel on the inside. My body has been through so much.

I want to love me, but I don't know where to begin. Do I love each piece in its broken state? Do I put the pieces back together and love the new creation?

How do I begin to embrace every piece of me; inside and out? How do I accept the ugliness inside? How do I accept the bruised outer shell?

I'm exhausted from the thought of it all.

Copy Cats

I know the look. "If she can teach this class, I know I can."

And eventually, they try to…to take over my class or seek to teach their own.

It used to bother me, but now I find it amusing, especially since eventually they all realize how difficult it is to teach any fitness class.

The memorizing routines, the teaching routines to others, the maintaining safety while teaching others, the modifications to meet the needs of a diverse class.

It's not that easy.

But, because I'm plus sized, I must be unhealthy, so I couldn't be working too hard up there, which means it doesn't take a lot to do what I do.

Then there's the attempt to try and out do me during class.

Kicking extra high, jumping up high like a damn fool, performing squats extra low, unaware of the damage it can cause to the body; teaching incorrect form to students.

Oh yea, that's right, I'm fat, so I don't know about health and wellness and safety in fitness.

I'm probably just unable to do those moves because I can't, you know with my size and all.

I'll admit it, some of it is my own insecurities about my body. Some of it too, is that in the past I questioned the abilities of instructors whose bodies didn't fit the societal image of health and wellness.

My internalized body shaming manifested itself in my thoughts about others. Although I was never cruel and judgmental in my words or actions, my thoughts were unkind. But, I was mostly unkind to myself.

Yes, I'm plus sized. I am in the best shape of my life. I am a fitness instructor, and a damned good one. See these curves. Judge them if you like. But, first, take my class!

ARM ANXIETY
(FROM CURVACEOUSLY FIT & HEALTHY BLOG)

I'm sure those in my weekly fitness classes may have noticed I always wear long sleeves or a jacket of some sorts during class. Well, that's because I have a love hate relationship with my arms.

The fat in our bodies is distributed differently based on a variety of factors. In my case, one of the areas where my fat hangs out is in my arms. Over the years, through weight losses and gains, I have become more and more self-conscious about my arms because of the fat deposits that are extremely noticeable when I raise them.

While a participant in fitness classes, I always wore short or no sleeve shirts. It was easy to disappear in the crowd where no one noticed my arms. However, as the instructor, I am center stage with all eyes on me. There are a lot of quick moves in my class, many of which require the use of arms; raising them up and down and moving them around.

As much as I enjoy teaching fitness classes, one of the initial reservations I had about becoming an instructor, was about baring my arms. What was I going to do? Then, the solution came to me.

When I pack my gym bag for each class I am always careful to include a workout top with sleeves. I even ordered two Tommie Copper sleeves so that if I would need to wear short sleeves, I could wear the Tommie Copper sleeves to hold in my arms. I thought I had covered all my bases.

Last week I packed one of my favorite mauve colored workout jackets to wear for class. This would prove to be a big mistake! Sure, I looked cute with my matching jacket, t-shirt and gym shoes, but I digress. It was after the second warm-up song that I noticed my hair and body were quickly becoming drenched with sweat.

My workouts are intense in my dance fitness class, and participants work up a good sweat, but there was no way I should have been sweating so profusely that early in the routine. Soon, I got over heated and started to feel a bit faint. My worst fear had been realized. I was going to have to take off my jacket and workout with just my t-shirt. I was so busy worrying about taking off my jacket that I missed a step during a routine. I recovered, but I knew I wasn't going to make it through the entire class wearing my beautiful mauve colored jacket.

The way I saw it, I had only two options. I could keep the jacket on, hide my arms, and pass out from heat exhaustion, or I could remove the jacket, bring my body temperature down, and unveil what I had managed to hide for six weeks.

I pulled the jacket over my head, laid it on the floor and began the next routine. I felt like I had just undressed in front of the entire class and was doing my class naked. I was hesitant to do arm moves, but I had no choice, so I continued, all the while wondering what my class was thinking about my arms. I was paranoid for the remainder of class. I thought the class was fixated on my arms. I kept looking through the mirror to see if I could notice any facial expressions that let on to their disgust of my fat arms. I couldn't keep this up. I was so busy concentrating on what the class was thinking about my arms that I was beginning to look like I was making up the routine on the fly.

When class ended, I quickly put back on my jacket. One of the participants in class was a young lady I'm quite close with who is a working professional, but was a student at the university, and comes to campus to attend group exercise class. I said to her, in a joking manner, "I'm sorry I had to expose you all to my arms." She looked at me confused and said, "What?" I explained that I had gotten overheated and had to take off my jacket. I told her I always wear long sleeves because my arms are fat. She looked at me and said, "I hadn't even noticed. I was just trying to keep up with you." There I was, missing steps, unable to concentrate, feeling paranoid, and she hadn't even noticed my arms.

What I took away from this experience was that I have a lot of work to do on learning to love my body, completely, with all its flaws. Loving my body means not being ashamed of it. It means respecting and caring for it. As I began to reflect on those things, I thought about I Corinthians 13. Specifically, I thought about verse 2, "And though I have the gift of prophecy, and understand all mysteries, and all knowledge; and though I have all faith, so that I could remove mountains, and have not love, I am nothing." My goal, you ask? It is to embrace my body by becoming Comfortably Curvaceous. Am I there yet? No, but I'm working on it.

CURVACEOUSLY BEAUTIFUL

Can I do it?

Can I look in the mirror and find something I love about this body?

Naked?

Bare?

Vulnerable?

Can I?

These curves of mine,

They are like a map.

I allow my finger tips to peruse the lines.

Where will they lead? On what journey will these lines take me?

The more I explore, the more curious I become.

I'm discovering something beautiful about the journey.

I'm discovering me; all of me. Every groove, curve, dimple, and stretch mark.

I'm not perfect, but I am beautiful.

I'll take that mirror now.

MIRROR, MIRROR
(FROM CURVACEOUSLY FIT & HEALTHY BLOG)

I recently took a trip to Montreal, Canada with two of my dearest friends. I've been to Toronto, but this was my first time in Montreal. Overall, it wasn't one of my best trips. It was cold, rainy and I ended up getting sick and staying in bed for one day of the trip.

However, the trip wasn't a total loss. It was during this trip that I began to see my body in a different way. We arrived at our hotel in downtown Montreal and were excited to get to our rooms after a long ordeal at the airport with my friend's luggage. Of course, the room was beautiful. The furnishings were amazing, the kitchen was quaint and there was ample closet space for my things.

At first glance of the bathroom I was quite pleased. However, upon further examination, I realized that the bathroom was small. There was a large, glass enclosed shower, but the toilet was rather close to the vanity. "I'll make it work", I thought.

It wasn't until I was preparing for bed and got ready to take a shower that I became mortified at what I had noticed earlier but hadn't given much thought; the glass enclosed shower was directly in front of the bathroom mirror! I thought, "oh, no, I have to look at my body while I'm in the shower!" This is not going to work. My only option was to not take a shower for the duration of the trip, and that wasn't going to happen. I thought, "You can do this. Just keep your eyes away from the mirror and you'll be fine."

Then, I thought about it, "Why don't you want to look at your naked body in the mirror?" The answer was because whenever I look at my body in the mirror at home when I'm getting dressed I always focus on the things I want to change. Before I allow myself to get too depressed, I get dressed quickly or just walk away from the mirror. But in the shower, where was I going to go?

When I first entered the shower, I tried to avoid eye contact with myself in the mirror. Then, I took a glance and shyly looked away. I got out of the shower, got dressed for bed, and lay there thinking about why it was so difficult for me to stare at my naked body and find something I like about it? I didn't have an answer to that one.

So, the next morning, I got in the shower and faced the mirror for much of the time. I looked at my body and thought about all the things my body can do and all that it is and focused less on what it is not. At the end of the day, it's my body. It's the only one I'll ever have, and it can do amazing things, like Zumba! This body is in the best shape it's ever been in my adult life. My body represents womanhood, femininity, strength and power, and that's nothing to be ashamed of. By the time I left Montreal I was feeling pretty good about my body; each curve, beauty mark, stretch mark, love handle and scar. It's all mine and I love it. Thanks, Montreal.

Untitled
(from Curvaceously Fit & Healthy Blog)

In May 2015, I made a decision that would change my life. I decided to become a fitness instructor for a popular Latin-inspired dance aerobics program. You're probably asking yourself, "How did that change your life?" Well, for a woman who has struggled with her weight since elementary school, becoming a fitness instructor was an amazing feat.

I can't take all the credit for my decision to become an instructor, though. My sister friend challenged me to be the change I wanted to see in my world. You see, I was complaining to her about how difficult it was to find a good instructor in my new neighborhood and she simply said, "Why don't you see about getting certified?" After laughing at the suggestion for several seconds, I started to really consider the possibility. I had been taking these Latin-inspired classes for about 3 years and absolutely loved it! Why not?

Of course, being the smarty that I am, I came up with several responses to that question. My first response was, "You are a plus size woman. No one will want to take a class from a plus size Zumba instructor." My second response was, "There is no way in hell you are going to make it through training! You are a plus sized woman." My third response was, "Maybe you could just complete the training for yourself. You don't have to do anything with it."

After I had come up with every excuse under the sun why I shouldn't take my friend's advice, I took a moment and forced myself to think about the reasons why I should. My first thought was, "You love these classes! This is the only exercise program you've done consistently, ever!" My second thought was, "This would be a great way for you to continue your exercise regime. Especially since as an instructor you'd have to practice and teach." My third thought was, "You are a plus size woman who enjoys going to fitness classes regularly. Imagine the other plus size women who may decide to exercise because there is a woman teaching the class whose body closely resembles their own."

And, with that, I went online, found a training class in my area, and registered. Now, I teach this high energy, dance inspired fitness class regularly. Yes, I am a plus sized woman. I have struggled with my weight all my adult life. However, today, I am in the best shape of my life. No cholesterol issues. No blood pressure issues. No diabetes. I eat well, most of the time, and I work out regularly. I have great friends and family, and I spend time regularly in reflection and with God. I am on a journey of acceptance. I am learning to love who I am, where I am, while remaining flexible and open to change.

5

FOOL ME ONCE, SHAME ON YOU

Romantic
Relationships
With Men

MISEDUCATION ABOUT LOVE

I gave loving you all the effort I had within me

Just like I do with everything.

I thought if I loved you enough and was a good woman

Everything would be perfect.

It's like with school,

If you successfully complete all the required courses, pass preliminary exams,

Write and defend the dissertation, then the degree is yours.

But, love ain't like getting no degree.

Cause if it was I'd have two PhDs.

INTUITION – CHEATING

As a woman, you know.

IT JUST HURTS

This hole in my heart mimics a hole in my spirit; a feeling of emptiness, of darkness.

I know it'll pass.

It just hurts so much.

This time I thought it'd be different.

You were everything he wasn't.

You said all the right things.

You smiled at me.

You looked at me as if I were the most beautiful woman in the world.

You saw me.

You touched me, in a way no man had touched me before.

And then, I awoke.

SHATTERED

I pretended. It's what I know.

Truth?

I was devastated.

I gave.

You.

Everything.

All I had.

You.

I wasn't enough.

All of me and it wasn't enough.

You. Had. Me. All of me.

But, it wasn't enough.

Me. Enough. All of me.

I gave.

You.

Enough.

Enough.

Truth?

I deserve better.

MY FLESH WAS WEAK, BUT MY SPIRIT...

I was hurting so bad with you.

I wanted to harm myself.

I should have harmed you.

Even through the hurt I never wanted to hurt you.

I didn't want you to feel the same pain you caused me.

I loved you like I never loved before.

I LOVED you!

You broke me...

financially, emotionally; bankrupt.

But my spirit, the part of me connected to God, held on and this hurt did pass.

I'm healed.

I'm free.

Undeniable Truth
(from Curvaceously Fit & Healthy Blog)

This has been a week of undeniable truths. And, while these truths were difficult to hear, after much reflection, I have accepted them and am moving forward.

The most hurtful truth came after I had a conversation with my ex-husband this week. We haven't spoken since our divorce was final in 2015. I had heard that he had gotten remarried only 6 months after our divorce. I held off processing it because I wasn't completely sure it was true. I guess I also didn't want to accept the fact that if he had gotten remarried so quickly, it was probably to his side chick.

During our conversation, he confirmed that he had indeed gotten remarried before the ink was dry on our divorce. He also, without knowing it, confirmed that it was the woman with whom he had been cheating. As he went on to explain to me why he got remarried, the undeniable truth that I had grappled with and hoped wasn't so, was confirmed. My ex-husband only married me because of my title and my income. That hurt. It hurt bad. And while he went on to tell me I was the best thing that ever happened to him, it was clear that he meant that in terms of what I brought to the table.

I loved my ex-husband. I poured everything I had into him and our marriage. I was intentional about being a loving, caring, and supportive wife. During our marriage there were decisions my husband made that confused me. How could you love someone and treat them this way? Well, now I know. His behavior was indicative of how he truly felt about me.

But, even with all that, I have forgiven him. What I understand and know to be true is that if a person doesn't love themselves they can never love you. My ex-husband doesn't love himself. He doesn't know how. As I reflect on what I learned about his family and his childhood, he was a hurt individual. And, hurt people, hurt people.

And, in forgiving him, I also forgave myself. Love is beautiful. *"Love is long suffering, and is kind; love envieth not; love vaunteth not itself, is not puffed up, doth not believe itself unseemly, seeketh not her own, is not easily provoked, thinketh no evil...love beareth all things, believeth all things, hopeth all things, endureth all things. Love never fails."*[1] And, because I love myself, I apply these principles to my life and how I treat myself. It is never a bad thing to love. It is what God expects of us.

I wish him well, and hope he finds peace and love within as I have.

---

[1] I Corinthians 13: 4 – 8. Holy Bible, New International Version.

What Does It All Mean?
(Random Thoughts and Questions)

All my romantic relationships have been long distance. What does that mean?

Why am I content with those types of relationships?

Even my closest friendships are long distance relationships.

Familial relationships? Mother? Distant (at least it was). Father? Distant.

The love I've experienced is never lasting; It comes for a visit then leaves.

Am I afraid that who I am can only be tolerated short-term?

When people come to visit I exhaust myself trying to make them comfortable. So much so, that I'm happy to see them leave.

Can I sustain that? Am I worried people won't like who they see, the real me?

Is it that I'm performing and can only keep up the performance for so long? Even my jobs tell a lot about my relationships.

Favorite job I've had? When I was recruiting. I was never really in the office.

Best part of all my jobs? Conferences. Leaving town, working and learning at my own pace.

Control. Is that what this is? I want to be in control?

I've been out of control in so many areas of my life? Food. Love.

Losing control is scary. I don't know why. It's not like we really control anything anyway.

JOURNAL ENTRY
MAY 2017

I was listening to *Piece It Together* by Zhané the other day, and I thought, how true. When do you know to give your love to someone again?

It's been two years, now, since my divorce, and while I'm in a much better place now than I was when my marriage was ending, there are times when I still feel sad that something that was supposed to last forever came to an end.

I told myself that the hurt of a divorce was just too much and that I wouldn't allow myself to ever feel that way about a partner again. Then, a few months after my divorce was finalized I met a gentleman who completely stole my heart. The story didn't end how I'd hoped, but how it usually does in these cases; girl meets boy, boy charms girl, girl is a bit hesitant, boy really charms girl, girl gives in to boy, boy leaves girl.

Now, I've met a new gentleman who is refreshingly different from past partners. We are just getting to know one another, but the urge in me to run for the hills has begun to crop up. Part of my heart and head says, "It's okay to take a chance. Life without risks isn't a life at all." But the other part of my heart and head says, "Girl, you remember what happened the last two times you let somebody in. You just don't get it!"

Here's what I know. I know that I've learned a lot from my past relationships. I know that I have grown as a woman; spiritually, mentally, and emotionally. I know that relationships are hard, but, like most things worth working hard for, the reward is great. I know that everything, e-v-e-r-y-t-h-I-n-g, in our lives happens for a reason.

So, I am going to continue to be prayerful, asking God to guide my thoughts and my actions. I am going to go slow, understanding that developing a friendship is most important. I am going to enjoy the process, allowing the butterflies to fly freely in my stomach. I am going to trust my instincts, my intuition, that spirit of discernment that God has given me. And, most importantly, I am going to continue to love me, knowing that to truly experience love, I must love myself with all my being.

DAYDREAMS OF YOU

As I lay here, I'm imagining you behind me.

I feel you so hard against me.

I'm so amazed by how willing I am to give you everything you want from me, including my body.

Caressing your back as you go deeper inside me.

I don't want you to stop.

I'll whisper your name in your ear.

You feel so good.

And when we're done, you hold me from behind like you did before we shared our bodies, and we both fall asleep.

What You Do to Me

Do you know what you do to me?

You got me wanting to do things I've been too afraid to do or not willing to do, but you.

You make me feel like I can live out my deepest fantasies with you and there would be no judgement to be had.

I say things to you I would never say to any other man.

My skin. You make me feel so comfortable in it.

I can explore with you. No restraints.

Let you do what you want. And. Still want more of you.

To know you in that way like only you know of yourself.

Deep inside me with your heart and your mind and your love.

I feel every inch of you.

You are me and I am you. One.

Lay with me forever like this.

Just like this.

PRESENT IN MY HEART

Laying here in your absence

I want your arms around me for comfort.

But, even in your absence I somehow feel your presence,
mostly in my heart.

That's the best place to feel it because it never leaves from
there.

So, I'll keep you in my heart where I know you'll be safe,
and where you're always just within my reach.

Before We Made Love (My Fantasy)

When I close my eyes, and listen to the melody of the music, I feel you next to me.

The deeper I allow my thoughts to go, the deeper I feel you inside me.

And deeper, even deeper still.

I gasp as I come back to reality.

My mind still reeling at the thought of you making love to me.

My body feels slightly satisfied.

I know what it needs to be complete.

You.

Lips to lips.

Tongue to mouth.

Body to body.

With each thrust, love to love.

If the thought of you satisfies me like this, I can only imagine...

AFTER WE MADE LOVE (MY REALITY)

The memories of your kisses dance across my lips.

So soft.

So sweet they were.

Passionate.

I lay my hands on your face to hold you there, in place.

I don't want you to stop.

I don't want this sweetness to end.

I feel like a woman, like God caused you to sleep and now
your rib I own.

I feel intimately known.

Call my name.

I won't run. I won't hide.

No leaves to cover us.

Free.

Unashamed.

This is a blessing.

To be loved this way by you.

To be known in this way by you.

You were so worth the wait.

You

Sometimes I just want to lay my head on your chest, smell your cologne, rub your chest hair.

Sometimes I just want to hear your heart beat, feel your breath as you kiss my forehead.

Sometimes, sometimes I just want to be held.

These things I need, I can't just have anyone give them to me.

I guess I just want to be loved, by you.

Yeah, I guess that's it.

YOU (PART II)

In sunshine and rain, I think about you.

When I'm happy or sad I think about you.

Just before I close my eyes at the end of the day and when I wake to a new dawn I think about you.

Is it the newness of love that keeps you on my mind or the awesomeness and beauty of you?

Whatever it is I enjoy it.

For a reason, a season, or a lifetime I don't know, but the blessing of your presence in my life will last until I take my last breath.

JOURNAL ENTRY
MAY 10, 2017

Relationships are hard. They're especially hard when you've had a string of failed ones, including a marriage that ended in a less than perfect way.

Loving is hard too. It's almost like you slit your arm open and hope that the person you cut yourself open for will do the same and you two heal together and the wound disappears like it never happened and you're happy you took the risk to expose your innermost being to the other person.

On the opposite side of the coin, the person could not only not open themselves up to you, but also could pour alcohol in the wound. It's the risk we take each time we enter that dating/courting stage of it. For some of us, those wounds resemble those of patients who cut themselves for psychological relief. It almost seems that way, that we cut ourselves open for love, but for no other reason than to know that we can still feel. That the numbness of life and love hasn't left us completely void of feeling, we want to feel alive, like we matter and exist.

As I'm learning to love myself like I didn't know I could, I am giving to myself what I thought I needed from a man. I give myself care and attention. I fight for me. I say kind things to myself and treat me to the things that make me happy. I pray and meditate with God; He is the head of my household. I know what satisfies me physically. I'm always satisfied.

I hold myself and feel the warmth of my own body. There is no disappointment, no wondering, I am content. I am kind and gentle and appreciate all the time I have alone with me. I feel young and smart and I reassure myself every day that I am enough. I am my everything in my relationship with myself.

Where have I been all my life. I was probably busy believing the lies from society, family, and peers that you are not complete unless you are someone's wife and mother. I was working toward the myth of the American Dream. The dream that's only made for those who designed it. It was never meant for me. I spent all that time chasing a lie. I unknowingly committed myself to a dream that was already deferred. But, we know all things work together for those that love the Lord, and I do love him/her.

So, these life lessons I take with me. And I have allowed these experiences to shape me, just like the potter molds his clay. This new creation, who loves her God-self, has accepted her greatness and her divine power.

6

I CANNOT BEAR THESE BURDENS ALONE

Spirituality

THE CHURCH

I was so confused about what it meant to have a relationship with God. I didn't grow up in a home where religion was practiced regularly, or spirituality was part of daily life.

We had the big bible on the coffee table like every other Black family in my neighborhood, but I rarely remember it being opened. I knew that God existed. Every Easter and Christmas we were dressed in the best clothes and would even attend church with one of my aunts; CME (Christmas, Mother's Day, and Easter) Christians, taking up the seats of the committed church going folks. That always got us dirty looks.

When I was old enough to make decisions on my own about religion, I began attending church and even got baptized. Throughout my young adulthood I attended a variety of Christian denominations trying to solidify my relationship with God and guarantee my place in heaven. I've been Baptist, Catholic, Seventh-Day Adventist, and non-denominational.

I was so naïve. I thought my relationship with God was based on how much time I contributed to the church and community through service. I didn't want to keep my talents to myself and disappoint God when he returned. I was always seeking understanding, so I read my bible and prayed daily. Still, I always felt like I was falling short. Sometimes the messages from church confused me more than they offered clarity.

I continued to seek God through his word and through the church. During that time, my mental health began to deteriorate. I was in a deep depression and was experiencing paralyzing anxiety. Then, just when I thought things couldn't get any worse, they did, and I was devastated.

THE PASTOR

"You should make an appointment with the pastor. I think he can help you with your depression. He's also a psychologist." My friend was a life saver. I had forgotten our pastor had a PhD in psychology and was a licensed counselor; a man of God and a therapist.

I contacted pastor and explained what was going on in my life. I explained how I sometimes feel that my soul is in turmoil. I feel lost. I disclosed that I had a history of depression, but had always been able to cope, now, my coping skills were failing me. I was so relieved when he said he could help me. We scheduled an appointment and I was so hopeful.

As I sat across from him, broken and weak, I waited for him to impart some wisdom, prayers, words of encouragement, something to help me begin healing. But instead, he began a commentary that shattered my broken spirit into unrecognizable pieces.

"I have always found dark-skinned women sexy. In my country we have a saying about dark women: sweet juices from the blackest berry. Your smile is beautiful. You know, if I weren't married I'd want to be with you."

My heart sank. As the tears welled in my eyes, the only words I could utter were, "but, pastor, my soul…"

THE OTHER PASTOR

I felt so dirty and ashamed. I thought, "What did I do to make a pastor say those things to me?" What was even more hurtful was that he took me back to all my childhood traumas of boys and men who had, themselves, heard stories about dark-skinned girls and promiscuity.

My saving grace in all this was that he had recently been removed from our church as pastor for a whole host of other reasons, so I no longer had to see him. The new pastor was more charismatic and his wife was very active in the church. In fact, she took a liking to me for some reason and I appreciated that. I also appreciated that she had called on an occasion or two to pray with and for me.

The pastor was friendly, and he also took an interest in me, especially since I had a leadership position in the church. Although I was flattered, I thought it was a little strange when he asked for my email address because he wanted to introduce me to his single brother. He thought we'd hit it off.

The flirtatious emails began almost immediately from the pastor followed by inappropriate comments and behavior at church. There was no brother; at least not one he wanted to introduce to me. I remember thinking, "My God, why? Why does this keep happening to me?" There was no answer.

Attending church became a source of anxiety for me, and eventually, I stopped attending. I didn't dare attend another church. Obviously, there was something I was doing to entice these men of God. Perhaps I'm just a temptress, a jezebel. That would explain the behaviors of my neighbor, the men on the stoop, the boys in the neighborhood. It wasn't their faults. It was me. I made them behave this way.

But, God

I know He exists. Just as sure as the earth spins on its axis, He exists.

My prayers had been few, my time with Him, in His word, well…

Church was a distant memory. That place and those people, I didn't care to remember.

But, God knows our hearts. He knows just what we need. I needed my faith to be restored.

That's when I met him, he was named after two books in the word.

The first book, ironically, instructions for the church and its leadership.

The second book, about carrying on the work of God that had already begun with His servant Paul.

He was such a God-fearing man. He prayed for me and with me.

The fruits of the spirit he did bear. I could see God in him.

The way he spoke to me. The way he looked at me and touched me. He was so gentle, so sweet.

He encouraged me and challenged me. He made me want to be better.

Now, my prayers are constant, my time with Him, in His word, daily.

My faith has been restored.

I thank the Lord for him.

UNTITLED
(LETTING GO)

Letting go is hard, but freeing.

Learning to allow God, the Universe, to conspire in my favor.

It's scary yet comforting.

Today I feel at peace.

Maybe it's because the sun was out all day.

Maybe it's because I paid some bills.

Maybe it's because I surrendered and came from behind the veil of "nothing's wrong" and "it's all good."

Maybe it's because even though I came from behind the veil, I still know God is in control.

Truth will always prevail, love will always win, and the light will always illuminate the dark!

This I know.

It's the Little Things

Gratitude.

I am grateful for so much.

Movement of my limbs: mobility and the ability to teach fitness classes

Empathy: the ability to understand the experiences of others and show compassion

Selflessness: giving of myself to others to be a blessing to them

Connection to a higher power: relationship with my creator God, the divine

Intellect and intelligence: the ability to reason and to learn

Friends: people who love me no matter what, not because they have to, but because they want to

Music: the ability to hear sound, the ability to connect with the experiences of others through music

My smile: my teeth and my mouth, being a blessing to others through my smile

My figure: my curves and edges, the confidence I feel in my clothes, shapeliness and flaws

Family: a reminder of my growth and development, a link to my past and my journey, learning and practicing forgiveness

It Don't Hurt Now

What Love Is

I love the way God loves me.

He cares for me.

He comforts me.

He makes decisions that are best for me.

It is through the love of God that I am learning how I should be loved by a man.

I should have done this before, but you don't know what you don't know.

EMPOWERED

When everything you need is right there

inside you

within your reach

but you are too exhausted from the woes of life

to grab hold of that piece of yourself that can rejuvenate

you.

Breathe.

Be still.

You can, and you will.

When it is time. When you are ready.

A New Day

I don't know that I've ever been this excited about stillness,
the prospect of nothingness.

It is the blank canvas of tomorrow that gives me peace.

WHEN WE ARE OBEDIENT, WE ARE BLESSED
JOURNAL ENTRY – AUGUST 2017

I remember it clearly. The day I received the email from a non-profit organization about applying to be a mentor. I printed out the application and set it aside to complete it later that day. When the time came to complete the application, I decided I didn't want a weekly responsibility of having to spend time with a kid; after all, I was trying to get my own life in order.

Just as I was about to toss the application in recycling I heard a soft voice say, "Complete the application and mail it in. Don't let your selfishness keep you from a blessing." So, being obedient, I completed the application and mailed it in. I was contacted for an interview and told there was a 6-week training. Again, I thought, I have stuff I need to do for myself. I don't have time to go through training for six weeks. And, again, that soft voice said, "You have the time to do this." So, I completed the training. A few months later I got a call that they had a match for me. In June 2017 I met my mentee.

These past couple of months with her have been some of the most emotional and trying months I've had in relation to another person. I have cried more for her than I have for anyone. I have spent more of my own weekly therapy time processing my feelings about her. I've never done that in therapy before.

Then, this morning, it hit me. My tears are not only for her, but for me as well. A few years ago, a therapist asked me to work on loving the little girl inside who never got the love and attention she needed. I wasn't sure how to do that. But, I realize now that it is through my mentee that I am working through my own issues of neglect and rejection.

She is 17 years old, but I refer to her as my little girl. I remember the first time I called her my little girl. She looked at me and said, "You know I'm not a little girl. I just turned 17." I said to her, "I know, but you're my little girl. Is that okay?" She looked down at her feet, and with a little smile shook her head yes. So now, whenever we're out I introduce her as my little girl and she always smiles.

What I'm learning is that she has never had the opportunity to be a little girl. She's had to grow up so quickly. She's experienced things no child should ever experience. When I listen to her, the pain, the hurt, the lack of self-esteem and love for self, I see myself and it hurts.

So, why do I let her drive my car when she asks? Or use my cell phone whenever she wants? Or choose the places we go even when I don't want to go? Because I understand. I understand.

I thank God for speaking to me on that day when I wanted to recycle my application. Although this process has been hard, I thank God for blessing me with her, and I thank him for using me as a blessing in her life. I am taking care of my little girl, my mentee, and the little girl inside me who needs healing, love, and attention.

WHEN WE ARE OBEDIENT, WE ARE BLESSED, PART II
JOURNAL ENTRY – JULY 2017

This past weekend I went to Atlanta to celebrate 40 years of life with one of my favorite friends. On my flight back, I was so tired and planned to put my earbuds in and sleep.

I settled into my seat in a row with two little girls, who didn't know one another, and were traveling for the first time alone. They seemed to be entertaining one another so I put on my earbuds in and began to listen to my music.

Then, as soon as I settled in for a nice quiet ride, I heard something inside me say, "Take those headphones off and engage with these little girls!"

Anyone who knows me, knows when I fly I don't like to be bothered. I definitely wasn't interested in entertaining children. But, I decided to be obedient.

The blessings we receive when we listen to that still, small voice is invaluable. I had the best time supporting these two young girls through their first flight alone, listening to them as they engaged in play, creating math problems for them so they could show me how smart they were, and listening to their dreams of playing in the WNBA and being a makeup artist.

This 10-year old and 8-year old didn't have any devices to occupy their time. They used good old fashion play to allow their imaginations to soar and to share their experiences thus far in life with me. It was truly a blessing and made my heart and spirit smile.

Wherever you are, Alyssa and Zaharia, I am so thankful that you engaged this 41-year old introvert and allowed me to be a part of your life for that brief hour and a half flight. You were a blessing.

In His Image

I find comfort in the fact that the God who created the heavens and the earth also created me.

The scripture says,

"For in him we live, we move, and have our being; as certain also as your own poets have said, For we are also his offspring."[1]

When the world around me is in chaos, and life isn't kind, I rest in this truth. I rest in Him.

[1] Acts 17:28. Holy Bible, King James Version.

PEACE LIKE A RIVER

It's 3:30 a.m. and I am wide awake. I know why. I feel it in my heart. God wants to speak to me.

It's at these times when it's completely silent and the darkest before the dawn that my heart and mind are most open, and my God knows that. He knows me.

He knows that I give my deposition tomorrow in my sexual assault case, and I'm nervous.

But my God, yes, my Lord, put a song in my heart; It Is Well with My Soul.

I love that hymn; it's one of my favorites. It speaks to me, and my Father knows that. He knows me.

And, he placed a scripture in my head; Exodus 33:22.

"And it shall come to pass, while My glory is passing by, that I will put you in the cleft of the rock and cover you with My hand until I have passed by."[1]

Yes, Lord. I trust you. I know you will protect me. And, whatever the outcome of this case, it is well with me and my soul. But, you knew that. You know me.

---

[1] Exodus 33:22. Holy Bible, King James Version.

IN THE MOMENT

As I've gotten older I've learned to appreciate every moment. I soak them up, allowing each one to linger on my tongue like my favorite taste. I know that in the next moment my present will be my past.

It's like that night at Pensacola Beach. The moon was beautiful, the waves of the gulf waters were so peaceful. I sat in the sand, under the moonlight, taking it all in, every crashing wave, every breath of mine, every thought.

I was thankful to be in that space, in those moments with God and his creations; the moon, the stars, the ocean, and me. Never wanting it to end, but fully aware that time was moving on and that the night, like all things, would have to come to an end.

And when it was over I was grateful that I had allowed myself to bask in those moments. They had passed but were forever imprinted in my heart. When I close my eyes and shut out everything else, I can hear the waves and feel the moonlight. I can be present with myself and my God.

CONCLUSION

I love Maya Angelou's poem *Still I Rise*. It reminds me that there is hope. All the situations in my life that I thought would surely break me helped me to be stronger. And, you too will be stronger. How do I know? I know because my personal experiences have taught me so. I rose from the ashes of a bad marriage. I rose from a fractured childhood and poverty. I rose from the ashes of molestation and a justice system that tried to shame me. Yes, like air, I rose!

I won't lie and tell you that you won't hurt. Sometimes my hurt was too much. I often contemplated suicide; looking for some relief from my pain. I felt like it was the end of the rope and it was only a matter of time before I came crashing to the floor after dangling for an eternity.

You must choose YOU! You must choose to take care of yourself; physically, emotionally, spiritually, and mentally. It will free you and will help you to teach others how to care for you. You must understand that you have more power than you realize. Once I realized that I am created in the image of God, the creator of the universe, and connected with my God-self, I realized and accepted my power. I embraced my inner strength and realized that I would be okay through whatever came my way. Pain is part of the process, but so is joy and peace. Honestly, that was what turned things around for me. Now, I know there is nothing I can't get through because I know from where my strength comes.

I found peace, and I know you can too. It will take some time and much effort on your part, but the reward, living your best life ever, is so worth it.

REFLECTION SECTION

SECTION ONE
REFLECTIONS

It Don't Hurt Now

_____

_____

_____

_____

_____

_____

_____

_____

_____

_____

_____

_____

_____

_____

_____

_____

_____

_____

_____

_____

_____

_____

_____

_____

_____

It Don't Hurt Now

SECTION TWO
REFLECTIONS

It Don't Hurt Now

_____

_____

_____

_____

_____

_____

_____

_____

_____

_____

_____

_____

_____

_____

_____

_____

_____

_____

_____

_____

_____

_____

_____

It Don't Hurt Now

SECTION THREE
REFLECTIONS

It Don't Hurt Now

It Don't Hurt Now

SECTION FOUR
REFLECTIONS

_____

_____

_____

_____

_____

_____

_____

_____

_____

_____

_____

_____

_____

_____

_____

_____

_____

_____

_____

_____

_____

_____

_____

_____

_____

_____

_____

_____

It Don't Hurt Now

_____
_____
_____
_____
_____
_____
_____
_____
_____
_____
_____
_____
_____
_____
_____
_____
_____
_____
_____
_____
_____
_____
_____
_____
_____
_____

It Don't Hurt Now

SECTION FIVE
REFLECTIONS

It Don't Hurt Now

It Don't Hurt Now

SECTION SIX
REFLECTIONS

It Don't Hurt Now

It Don't Hurt Now

ABOUT THE AUTHOR

Christie Ann Cruise, PhD is a social justice educator and trainer with a passion for empowering women and girls to find their voices in a society that all too often silences them. Dr. Cruise's passion has led her to serve as a mentor with the Reach & Rise Program of the Gateway Region YMCA, an advisory board member for Nia Kuumba African and African American Women's Spirituality Center, and treasurer for the Young Ambassadors of the YWCA of Metro St. Louis.

As an Athletics and Fitness Association of America (AFAA) certified group instructor and a licensed Zumba™ instructor, Dr. Cruise advocates for women and girls of all shapes to use fitness as a tool to develop positive body image.

Dr. Cruise's passion for the empowerment of women and girls is fueled by her own experiences with childhood molestation and adult sexual assault. After her marriage of 7 years ended, she began her journey of self-discovery to restore the identity she relinquished, and of self-love to recover the self-esteem she lost. Dr. Cruise has found her voice and the strength to share her story through spirituality and her connection to God.

Cruise received a Bachelor of Science degree in Food Science from the University of Illinois at Urbana-Champaign, a Master of Science degree in College Student Affairs from Eastern Illinois University, and a PhD in Higher Education Administration from Bowling Green State University.

info@christieanncruise.com
www.christieanncruise.com
https://christiec.zumba.com

Made in the USA
Las Vegas, NV
01 September 2021

29341827R00085